CAMBRIDGE

Official Cambridge Exam Preparation

FUNSkills

Student's Book 1

Claire Medwell • Adam Scott

Cambridge University Press
www.cambridge.org/elt

Cambridge Assessment English
www.cambridgeenglish.org

Information on this title: www.cambridge.org/9781108582148

First published 2020

20 19 18 17 16 15 14 13 12 11 10 9 8

Printed in Great Britain by Ashford Colour Press Ltd.

A catalogue record for this publication is available from the British Library

ISBN 978-1-108-58214-8 Student's Book and Home Booklet with Online Activities

Contents

Map of the book

Unit	Topic	Skills focus	Can do	
1 School page 6	Classroom objects Greetings and introductions	**Listening** Listen for names and descriptions and draw lines to match names to people in pictures	Understand very simple spoken descriptions	Song
2 Family and friends page 10	Family	**Listening** Listen and write numbers 1–20 and family members	Understand and write numbers 1–20 Understand and write the names for family members	
Review Units 1–2 *page 14*				
3 Move your body! page 16	Body parts Colours	**Reading and writing** Write a simple description using a gapped text **Speaking** Answer questions about a picture with short answers	Write a simple description using *has got* and *likes* Understand simple questions and give simple answers	Think Big Chant
4 At the farm page 20	Animals	**Reading and Writing** Read short sentences and recognise key words Tick or cross to show if a sentence is true or false	Read and understand short, simple words and names of farm animals and pets	Chant
Review Units 3–4 *page 24*				
5 Clothes page 26	Clothes	**Reading and Writing** Write *yes* or *no* to indicate if a picture and word match	Understand very basic descriptions of items of clothing (number, colour, etc.)	Think Big
6 Food and drink page 30	Food Drink Meals	**Reading and Writing** Unjumble and write words to match a picture Write words correctly	Spell some simple words correctly	Song Think Big
Review Units 5–6 *page 34*				

1 School

❶ **Complete the classroom words.**

❷ **Look and read. Write *yes* or *no*.**

Example The bookcase is red. *yes*

1 The cupboard is green. ______
2 The board is black. ______
3 The wall is pink. ______
4 The desk is green. ______
5 The tablet is blue. ______

3 Look at the pictures. Choose the correct word.

Example This is a  **board / bookcase.**

1 This is a  **cupboard / desk.**

2 These are  **posters / windows.**

3 This is a  **wall / floor.**

4 This is a  **classroom / playground.**

4 Listen and draw lines.

Sam

Alice

Bill

Hugo

Lucy

Sue

5 Listen to the song and do the actions. See page 66.

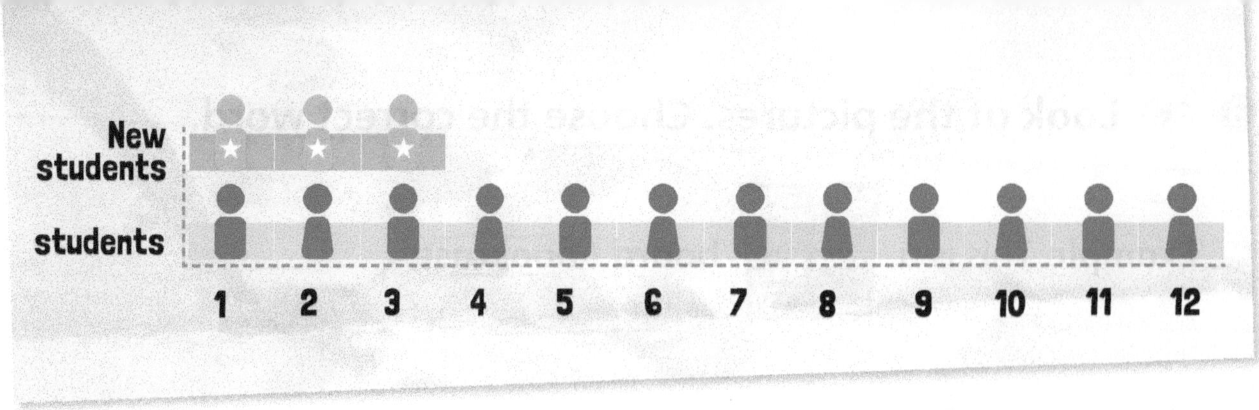

1 Look and complete.

There are ________ students in the class.

There are ________ new students in the class.

2 04 Listen and complete.

3 Ask and answer with a friend.

A Hello! I'm new in class.

B What's your name?

A Omer.

B How do you spell that?

A O–M–E–R.

4 Look at the photos. Do you play these games? Ask and answer with a friend.

Do you play tag?

5 05 Listen and number the photos.

6 What is your favourite playground game? Draw a picture and talk to a friend about it.

My favourite playground game is ________ .

2 Family and friends

1 Look at the photos. Talk to a friend. Where do you think the people live?

2 06 Listen and number the photos 1–4.

3 07 Look and write. Listen and check.

A Hello, my name's Angavu.
There are ___3___ people in my family:
________ children and
________ woman.

B Hello, my name's Miguel.
There are ________ people in my family:
________ women,
________ man,
________ girls and
________ boy!

C Hello, my name's Tivi.
There are ________ people in my family:
________ children,
________ man and
________ women.

D Hello, my name's Ben.
There are ________ people in my family:
________ man and
________ boy, me!

4 Read and choose.

Example There are four **persons** / **people** in my family.

1 There is one **child** / **children** in my family. It's me!

2 There are two **woman** / **women** in my family.

3 There are three **men** / **man** in my family.

5 Complete the family words. What's the new word?

g r a n d ☐ a t h e r
☐ u n t
s i s ☐ e r
b r o t ☐ e r
m o t h ☐ r
g ☐ a n d m o t h e r

6 Listen for the er sound. Choose the picture that is different.

Example

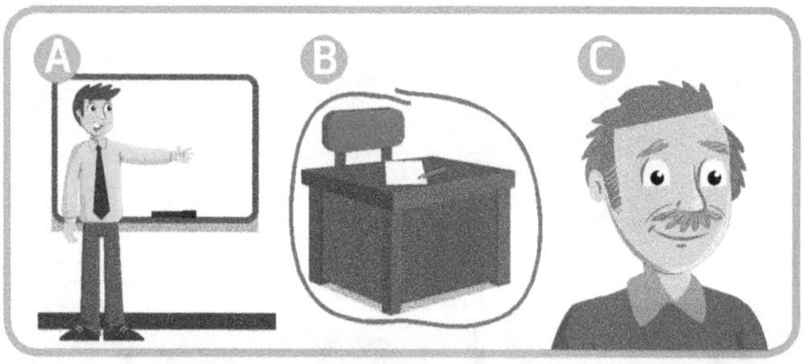

1 Ask and answer with a friend.

2 Read about Carmen's family. Draw a picture of them.

Carmen's family and pets

My name's Carmen! I've got a big family. I've got three sisters and one baby brother. We all live with my mum, dad, grandmother and grandfather in a big house in the city. We've got some pets too!

Our dog's name is Buddy. He likes playing in the garden. And our cat's name is Snowy. Buddy and Snowy are good friends!

3 Complete the sentences.

Example I'm Carmen and this is my *city*.

1 This is my ________ .

2 These are our ________ .

3 This is my ________ .

4 These are my ________ .

1

2

3

4

4 Complete the pictures of your family. Write about your family.

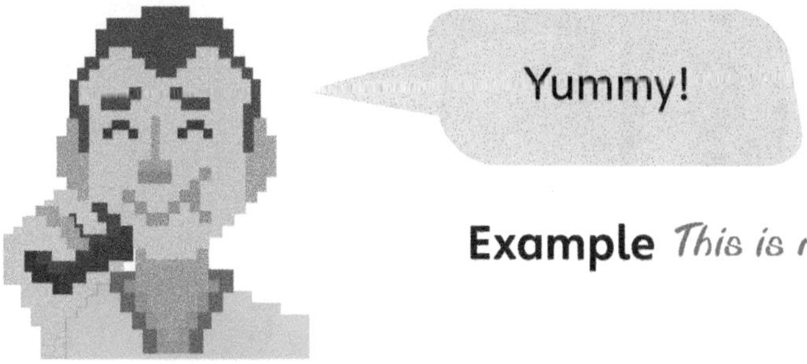

Example *This is my father. He likes chocolate.*

This is ______________________.

__________ likes ______________________.

This is ______________________.

__________ likes ______________________.

This is ______________________.

__________ likes ______________________.

This is ______________________.

__________ likes ______________________.

5 Talk to a friend about your family.

Review Unit 1

Skills: Reading, Speaking

1 Draw and write the words.

1 b ___ ___ ___ d
2 b ___ ___ k ___ ___ ___ e
3 d ___ ___ k
4 w ___ ___ d ___ w
5 c ___ p ___ ___ ___ ___ d
6 c ___ ___ p ___ ___ ___ r
7 p ___ ___ t ___ r

Mark: ___ / 7

2 Read and colour.

1 This is a blue cupboard.

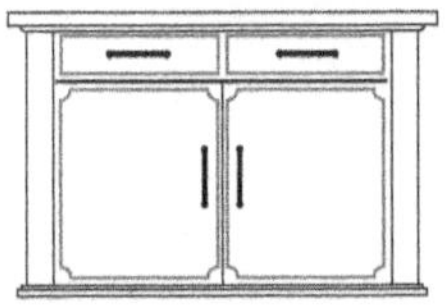

2 These are pink tablets.

3 This is a red desk.

Mark: ___ / 5

4 These are yellow bookcases.

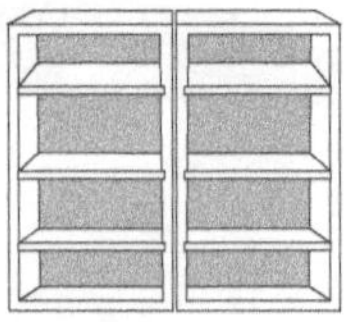

5 This is a black computer.

3 Look around your classroom. Write the number. Check with a friend.

My classroom

1 ________ cupboard(s)	3 ________ board(s)	6 ________ window(s)
2 ________ desk(s)	4 ________ computer(s)	7 ________ wall(s)
	5 ________ poster(s)	8 ________ bookcase(s)

How many cupboards are there?

There are two cupboards.

Mark: ___ / 8

Total: ___ ___ / 20

Skills: Reading, Listening

1 Complete the word puzzle.
Find the words in the box.

n	e	f	s	b	n	p	b	l	l	g	e	n	e
g	r	a	n	d	f	a	t	h	e	r	a	m	y
m	u	t	p	b	y	p	c	k	l	a	n	a	s
g	a	h	p	r	r	m	i	s	n	n	r	b	i
r	h	e	l	s	a	e	u	a	i	d	r	a	s
r	a	r	i	n	r	e	a	g	a	m	i	e	t
p	c	s	u	o	n	m	c	k	l	o	p	t	e
e	a	a	t	m	r	r	g	m	o	t	h	e	r
s	e	e	e	y	i	a	m	k	e	h	g	a	k
u	p	i	n	i	b	r	o	t	h	e	r	o	m
p	y	o	s	e	w	l	r	y	r	r	e	p	g

Mark: ___ / 6

2 09 Listen and tick (✓) the correct picture.

A

B

Mark: ___ / 2

3 Read about Jesse's family.
Write the words from the box.

women brother six father
grandmother men children

There are (1) __________ people in my family. There are two (2) __________ , my mother and my (3) __________ . And there are two (4) __________ , my (5) __________ and my grandfather. There are two (6) __________ . Look there I am! I'm standing next to my (7) __________ .

Mark: ___ / 7

Total: ___ ___ / 15

3 Move your body!

❶ Write the body parts.

arms | body | feet | hands | head | legs

❷ 10 Listen and say the words.

3 Listen and colour the body parts in task 1.

4 Look and listen. Write the numbers next to the robots.

1 Dan

2 Sue

3 May

5 Look and talk to a friend.

THINK BIG

What can robots do?

1 Draw a robot.

2 Write about your robot.

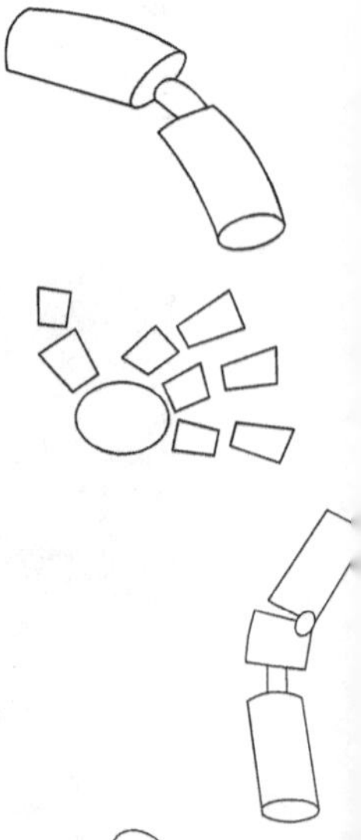

Here's my robot! Its name is ______________________ .

My robot has got ______________________ and ______________________ .

It has got ______________________ and ______________________ .

It has got a ______________________ and a ______________________ .

My robot likes ______________________ .

3 Talk to a friend about your robot. Ask and answer questions.

This is my robot. Its name is Skoolio.

Has your robot got yellow arms?

No, it hasn't. It's got blue arms.

4 13 Listen and chant.

Look at my robot!
It's got three arms and four legs.
Has it got small feet? Yes, it has!

This is my robot.
I like it a lot!
Look at my robot!

It likes cleaning. It likes painting.
It likes walking and talking.
This is my robot. I like it a lot!

5 Look. Ask and answer the questions.

1 How many children are there?
2 How many posters are there?
3 What's the teacher doing?
4 What do you do in class?

4 At the farm

1 Look. Where does Ameena live? What animals can you see?

2 Write the words. Match them to the animals.

ocw c o w

1 kcud _ _ _ _

2 meuso _ _ _ _ _

3 soher _ _ _ _ _

4 ecnhcik _ _ _ _ _ _ _

5 ogat _ _ _ _

3 How many animals are there in task 1? Count and write.

There's ...	There are ...
a goat	*two horses*
1 ________	3 ________
2 ________	4 ________

4 Look at the picture in task 1 again. Read and put a tick (✓) or a cross (✗) in the box.

Example There are two horses. ☑ ✓

1 There's a mouse. ☐
2 There are three cows. ☐
3 There are four chickens. ☐
4 There's a cat. ☐
5 There are two goats. ☐
6 There are three ducks. ☐

5 Look. Ask and answer with a friend.

What is it?

It's a goat.

What colour is it?

It's green!

1 Look. Ask and answer questions about the picture.

2 Look and read. Put a tick (✓) or a cross (✗) in the box.

Example  These are cows. ✗

1  This is a cat. ☐

2  These are horses. ☐

3  These are lizards. ☐

4  This is a frog. ☐

5  This is a sheep. ☐

③ 14 **Listen to Jacob talking about pets. Circle the correct words.**

1 What is your favourite pet? **goat / cat**
2 What does it eat? **fish / vegetables**
3 What does it like? **sleeping / running**
4 Where does it sleep? **under a tree / in the hall**

④ **Draw your favourite animal.**

⑤ **Talk to a friend about your favourite animal.**

My favourite animal is ...
It likes ... It sleeps ...

Skills: Reading, Writing

1 Read and draw.

My doll is called Hugo. He's got blue arms and legs, and a yellow body. He's got an orange head, with black hair and green eyes. He's got black hands and red feet.

My monster is Suzy. She has got a brown face with long orange hair. She has got a green body, purple arms and red hands. She has got white legs and blue feet.

Mark: ___ / 8

2 Look and write.

My robot has got green **1** a__________ , blue **2** h__________ and orange **3** f__________. It has got a red **4** f__________ , yellow **5** h__________ , green **6** l__________ and a big smile!

Mark: ___ / 6

3 Look and talk to a friend.

She's got black feet and brown legs. She's got pink ears.

It's Clara!

Mark: ___ / 6

Total: ___ / 20

Skills: Writing, Listening, Speaking

1 Match.

1	mou	A	ken
2	go	B	key
3	hors	C	at
4	chic	D	ard
5	don	E	e
6	liz	F	se

Mark: ___ / 6

2 15 Listen and number the photos.

Mark: ___ / 5

3 Look and talk to a friend.

Mark: ___ / 9

Total: ___ / 20

There are two cows in the picture.

Yes!

5 Clothes

1 Look at Frankie's bedroom. Tick (✓) the clothes you can see.

1 shoes	☐	2 hat	☐	3 shirt	☐	4 shorts	☐
5 jeans	☐	6 T-shirt	☐	7 skirt	☐	8 socks	☐

2 Where is Frankie's ballet shoe? Point to the picture and tell your friend.

3 Look at the picture in task 1 again. Answer the questions with one word.

Example How many shirts can you see? *three*

1 What colour are Frankie's ballet shoes? ________

2 Can you see a hat? ________

3 How many skirts are there? ________

4 Is Frankie's ballet shoe on the chair? ________

4 Look at the pictures and the letters. Write the words.

Example

T-shirt

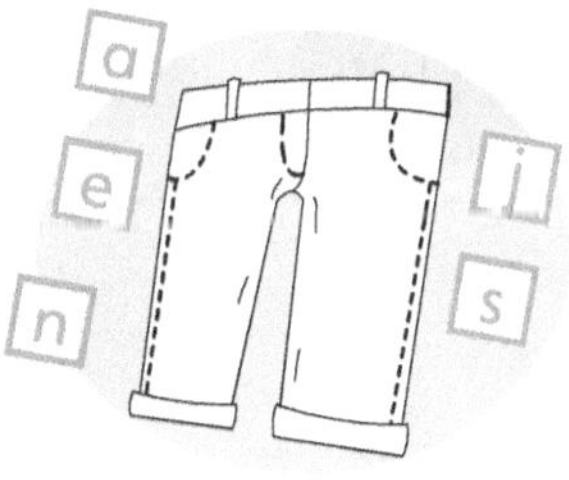

1 ______

2 ______

3 ______

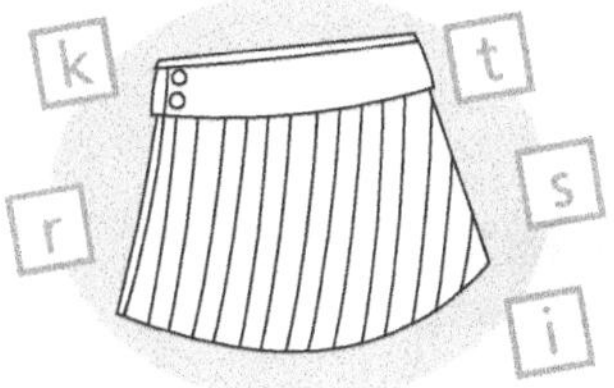

4 ______

5 ______

6 ______

5 Listen and chant. See page 67.

16

6 Read and look. Write yes or no.

Example There's a red T-shirt. yes

1 There are two black boots. ______

2 The baseball cap is under the jacket. ______

3 There are three jackets. ______

4 The shorts are new. ______

5 The trousers are blue. ______

1 Look at the photos. Ask and answer with a friend.

Which clothes do you like?

THINK BIG

2 17 Listen and number the photos in task 1.

3 Look at the photos in task 1 again. Write the words.

1 The girl is wearing red t*rousers*______ and a black h______ .
2 She is wearing a white j______ and g______ .
3 The boy is wearing an orange T-______ and a red and w______ helmet.
4 The girl is wearing a yellow T-______ and red sh______ .

4 Draw clothes for Captain Zoom and Max.

5 Write about the clothes in task 4.

Captain Zoom is wearing ______________________________
____.

Max is wearing ______________________________
____.

6 Talk to a friend about the clothes in task 4.

He is wearing red and white socks.

7 Play a game. Guess who?

6 Food and drink

1 breakfast

2 lunch

3 dinner

1 **Look at the photos. Tell a friend what food and drink you can see.**

2 [18] **Listen, point and sing. See page 67.**

3 **Look at the pictures. Write the words.**

Example

 *m i l k*

1  _ _ _ _

2  _ _ _ _ _

3  _ _ _ _

4  _ _ _ _ _

5 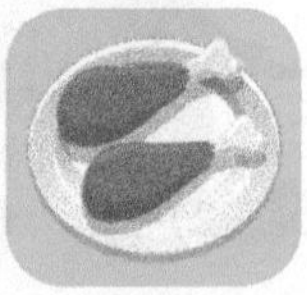 _ _ _ _ _ _ _

4 Draw your favourite food for breakfast, lunch and dinner. Tell a friend about your food.

breakfast	lunch	dinner

5 19 Listen to Hugo and Alice talking about the food they like and love. Put a tick (✓) for like. Draw a heart (♥) for love.

Hugo							
Alice							
Me							

6 Complete the 'Me' part in task 5. Talk to a friend. Do you like the same things?

THINK BIG

1 Look at the photos. Tick the food that's good (✓) for you. Cross the food that's bad (✗) for you.

2 Read and write the food.

1 I'm round and green.
I'm an ________ .

2 I'm a vegetable.
I'm long and orange.
I'm a ________ .

3 I'm a drink. I'm white.
I come from cows.
I'm ________ .

4 I'm a fruit. I'm long and yellow.
I'm a ... ________ .

❸ Look at the photos and write the words.

1 I've got b_ _ _ _ _ hair.
2 I've got k_ _ _ _ eyes.
3 I've got an a_ _ _ _ _ mouth.
4 I've got o_ _ _ _ _ ears
and a b_ _ _ _ _ nose!

5 I've got two b_ _ _ _ _ eyes.
6 I've got a c_ _ _ _ _
beak and a_ _ _ _ _ wings!

❹ Draw a plate with food that's good for you.

❺ Talk to a friend about your plate.

Skills: Reading and Writing

1 Look and write.

What do you wear when it's sunny?

1 ___ ___ orts

2 ___ - ___ ___ irt

3 ___ ap

What do you wear when it's raining?

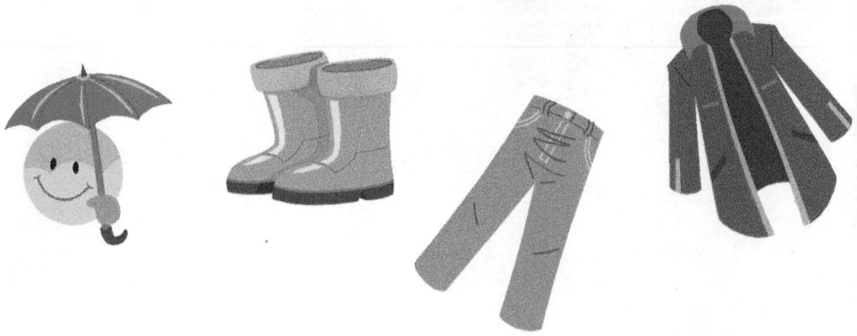

4 ___ ___ ots

5 ___ ___ ans

6 ___ ___ cket

Mark: ___ / 6

2 Read, draw and colour.

Mark: ___ / 6

3 Write about you.

Hi! My name's ______________________ .
I wear ______________________
____
______________________ .

Mark: ___ / 8

Total: ___ ___ / 20

Skills: Listening, Reading, Speaking

1 20 **Listen and number the photos.**

A

B

C

D

Mark: ___ / 4

2 **Look at the photos in task 1 again. Read and match the sentences to the photos. Write A-D.**

1 I like carrots. ☐

2 I like bananas. ☐

3 I like watermelon. ☐

4 I like apples. ☐

Mark: ___ / 4

3 **Make juice with three types of fruit. Draw and tell a friend.**

Mark: ___ / 4

Total: ___ ___ / 12

7 Fun! Cool! Great!

1 Look at the picture. What can you see? Tick (✓) the boxes.

a book	☐	a balloon	✓	trees	☐	a hat	☐
a lizard	☐	an ice cream	☐	a ball	☐	boots	☐

2 Read. Look at the picture in task 1 and find Toby.

My name is Toby and I'm at Cool Park! There are lots of great rides and lots of **happy** children. I've got **short** brown hair. I've got a **big** balloon and I'm wearing a paper hat. My T-shirt is **dirty**. Can you find me?

3 Write the adjectives from task 2 next to their opposites.

1 long ________
2 sad ________
3 clean ________
4 small ________

4 Look at the map of Cool Park. Where do you want to go? Write sentences.

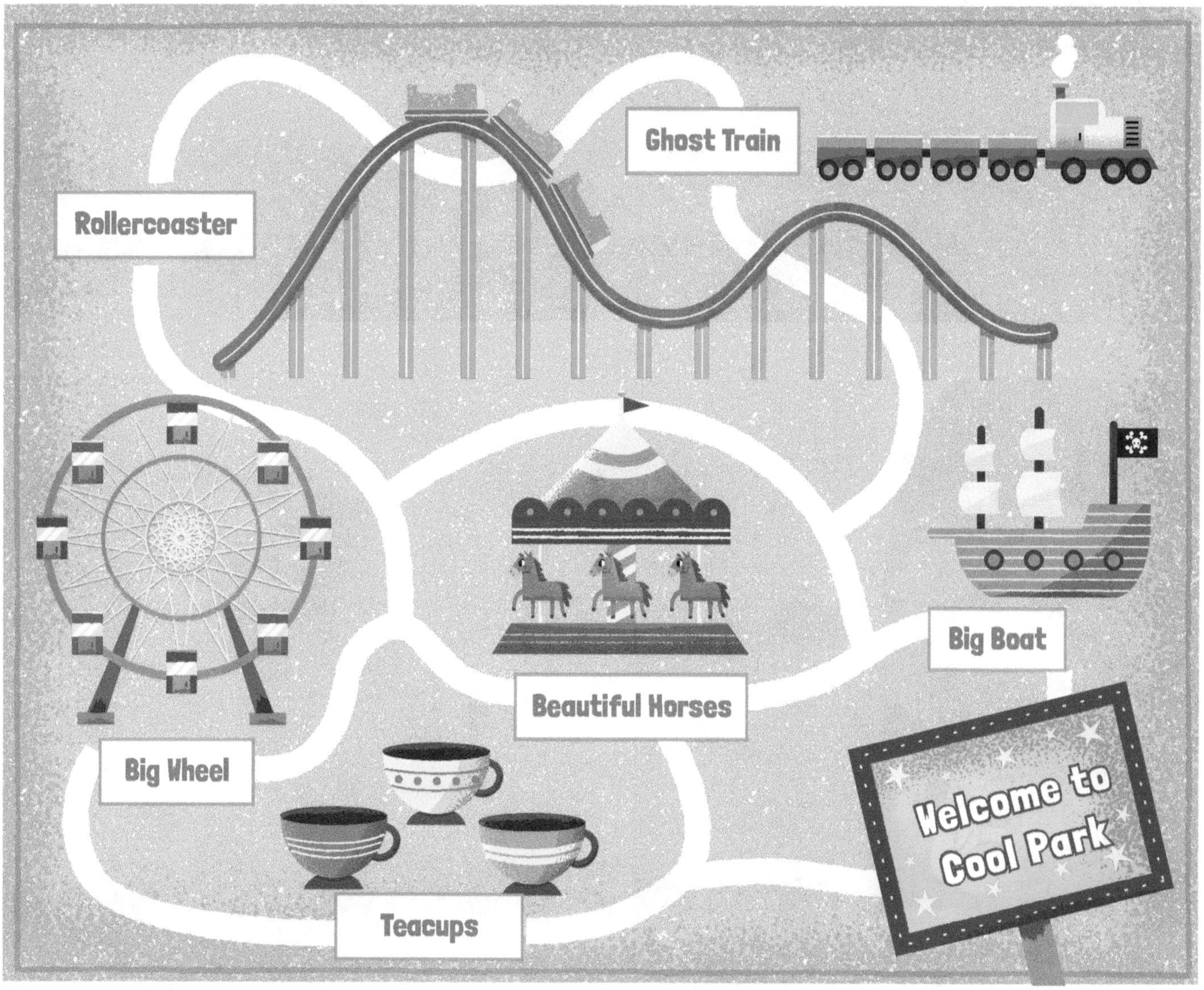

Example I want to go on the *Big Boat*. It's *fun*.

1 I want to go on ________________ . It's ________ .
2 I don't want to go on ________________ . It's ________ .

1 Look at the pictures. Where are the family? Are they happy?

2 Circle the correct words to make questions about the pictures in task 1.

Picture 1

1 *How* / *How many* children are there?
there are ________________

2 *Who* / *What* are the children with?
their ________________

3 *What* / *Who* is the monster holding?
a ________________

Picture 2

4 *How old* / *What colour* is mum's hair?
it is ________________

5 *How* / *What* is Dad doing?
taking a ________________

6 *Where* / *Who* is not happy?
the ________________

3 Now complete the answers in task 2. Use these words.

boy two blue lamp photo dad

4 21 Listen and tick (✓) the correct picture.

1  ☐  ☐

2  ☐  ☐

3  ☐  ☐

8 Sports

1 (22) **Look and listen. Point to the sports. Complete the words.**

1 b _ s _ b _ ll
2 b _ sk _ tb _ ll
3 f _ _ tb _ ll
4 h _ ck _ _
5 j _ mp _ ng
6 sk _ t _ b _ _ rd _ ng
7 sw _ mm _ ng
8 t _ bl _ t _ nn _ s
9 t _ nn _ s

2 **Tick (✓) the sports you play. Cross (✗) the sports you don't play. Talk to a friend.**

3 (23) **Listen again. How many syllables does each word have? Which one is stressed?**

4 Read and match.

Example I'm kicking a ball.

1 I'm swimming.
2 I'm bouncing a ball.
3 I'm holding a bat.
4 I'm riding a skateboard.

5 24 Listen and tick (✓) the box.

1 What is Jo riding?

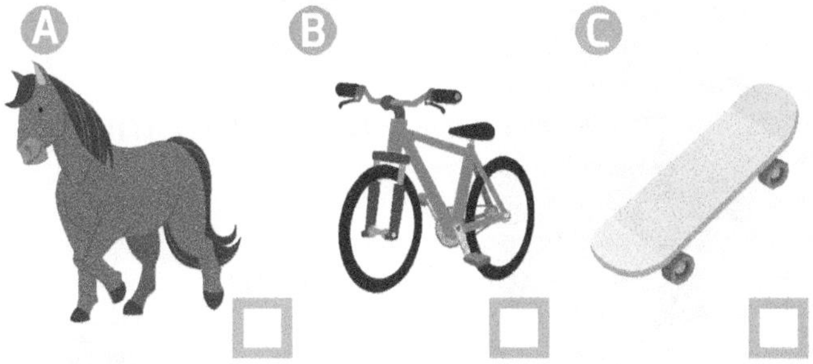

2 What is Kim playing?

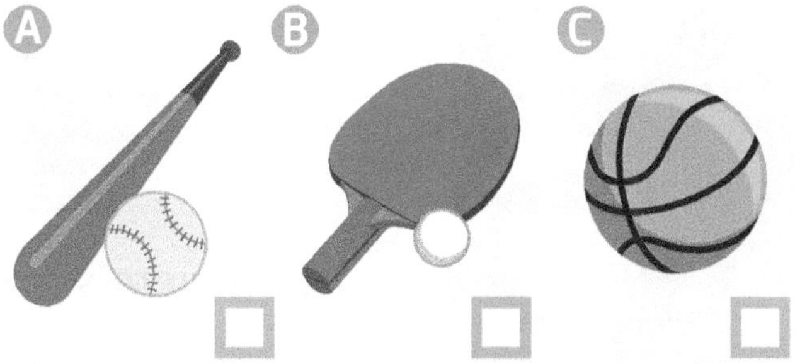

3 What is Nick holding?

4 What is Pat doing?

6 Mime a sport. Ask and answer with a friend.

7 25 Sing and act out. See page 68.

1 Look and write.

Example

I can't find my teddy.
[tyded]

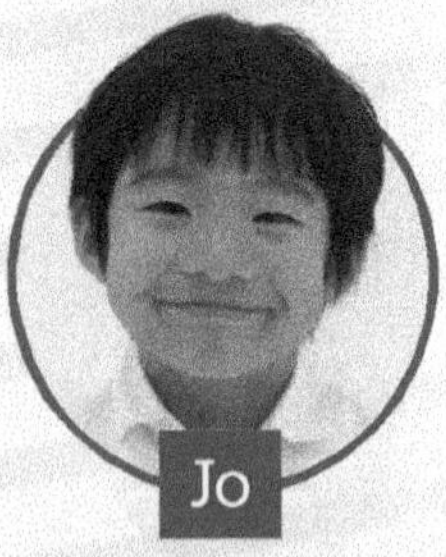

1 Where's my ________ ?
[rboto]

2 I want my ________ .
[oldl]

3 Help me find my ________ .
[ialne]

4 I want my ________ .
[labl]

5 Where's my ________ .
[otmensr]

2 26 Listen and write the first letter of the toy next to each picture. There is one example.

3 Read and match.

1 **Whose** is the teddy?
Where is it?

2 **Where** is the ball?
Whose is it?

A It's **next to** the flowers.
B It's Sam'**s**.
C It's Kim'**s**.
D It's **in** the sandpit.

4 Talk about the toys in task 1. Ask and answer with a friend.

Whose is the … ?

Where is it?

It's …'s.

It's …

5 Choose and write five toys. Read where to put each toy. Draw it in that place.

the teddy

is on the table.

______

is under the chair.

______

is next to the window.

______

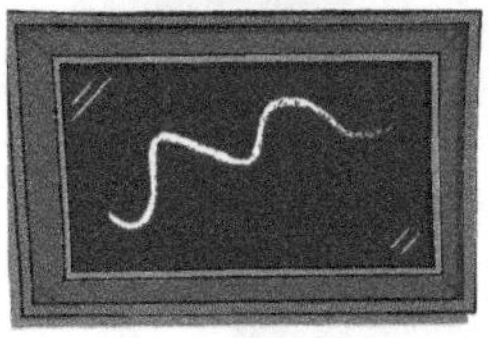

is in front of the board.

______

is behind the door.

______

is in the cupboard.

Review Unit 7

Skills: Reading, Writing

1 Look at the picture. What can you see? Choose the correct words.

Example happy / sad children

1. plastic / paper cups
2. small / big cake
3. quiet / noisy party
4. coloured / black clothes
5. boring / fun party
6. beautiful / ugly balloons

Mark: ___ / 6

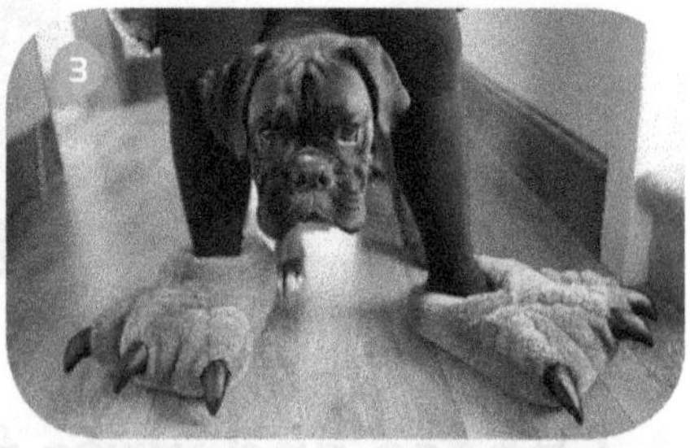

2 Look and read. Write yes or no.

1. The boy is shouting. ________
2. The girl is happy. ________
3. The boy is wearing a scary eye patch. ________
4. It is a cat. ________
5. The girl can't see. ________
6. They are wearing hats. ________

Mark: ___ / 6

3 Look and write.

long	happy	eye masks	boat	black	red

The boys are on the ________ . They look ________ . Three boys are wearing ________ pirate's hats and one boy is wearing a ________ hat. Two boys are wearing ________ and one is holding a ________ sword.

Mark: ___ / 6

Total: ___ / 18

Skills: Writing, Reading, Speaking

1 Write the words for toys and sports.

dytde lodl kocehy elnai btsablelak bsabella trboo mswingmi

1 ________ 2 ________ 3 ________ 4 ________

5 ________ 6 ________ 7 ________ 8 ________

Mark: ___ / 8

2 Read and draw.

Where's my doll? Your doll is next to the horse.

Where's my ball? Your ball is under the window.

Where's my skateboard? Your skateboard is on the floor.

Where's my monster? Your monster is on the horse.

Where's my car? Your car is on the box.

Mark: ___ / 5

3 Look. Ask and answer with a friend.

Kim

Nick

Joe

Sam

Pat

Alex

Ben

Mark: ___ / 7

Total: ___ ___ / 20

9 Transport

1 Look at the picture. What types of transport can you see? Tell a friend.

2 Circle the transport words. Write them in the picture in task 1.

❸ 27 **How do our favourite characters go to the beach? Listen and match.**

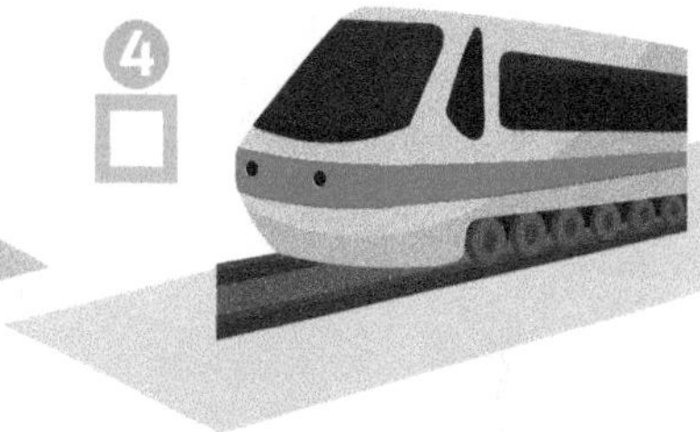

❹ **Write sentences about the characters in task 3.**

Example Leon goes to the beach ___*by train*___ .

1 Max goes to the beach ______________ .

2 Piper goes ______________ .

3 Nedda ______________ .

❺ **How do you go to different places? Ask and answer with a friend.**

1 (28) Listen and chant. Write the words.

drive **fly** **walk** **ride**

Hurry, hurry
Don't be late!
It's time to go
to school

beep beep
______ in a car

ding
______ a bike

ha ha
______ with friends too

______ a horse
clip clop

brum
______ a bus

whoosh
______ in a blue plane

Hurry, hurry
Don't be late!
It's time to go
to school

2 Look and read. Tick (✓) the correct sentence.

1

A He goes to school in a car. ☐

B He rides to school on a motorbike. ☐

2

A She rides her motorbike to work. ☐

B She drives her lorry to work. ☐

3

A They ride their bikes to the beach. ☐

B They go to the beach by bus. ☐

4

A We fly on a plane to different countries. ☐

B We fly on a helicopter to different countries. ☐

3 **Read. Choose words and complete.**

pets toys classmates ~~school~~ food

Some children go to ___school___ by car or they walk there. I take the bus with my (1) __________ because it's fun. We talk and sing. We can't have any (2) __________ or drinks on the bus. And we can't bring our (3) __________ like cats and dogs. But we can bring our (4) __________ . I've got my ball.

4 **Which children are safe? Talk to a friend. Tick (✓) the boxes.**

1

 ☐  ☐

2

 ☐  ☐

3

 ☐  ☐

THINK BIG

Are you safe?

10 House

1 Read and match.

Hi! I'm Manuel and this is my sister Clara. We live in a flat. We can see all the city from the flat!

Hi! My name's Zlav. I live in an apartment with my family and pets!

Hello, I'm Aiko. I live in a house with my mother and grandmother.

house

flat

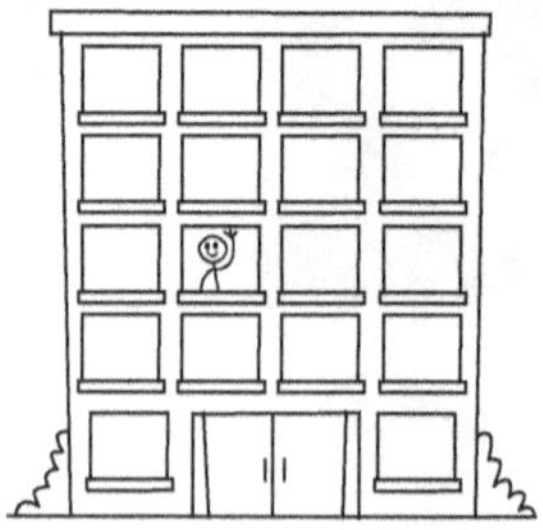

apartment

2 Draw your home. Write.

Hi! My name's ______________________.

I live ______________________

____

____

❸ Number the parts of the house.

1 living room   2 bedroom   3 bathroom   4 dining room   5 kitchen

❹ Look and complete.

Example  b _a_ t _h_

1 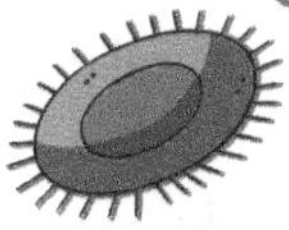 __ a __

2  mi __ ro __

3 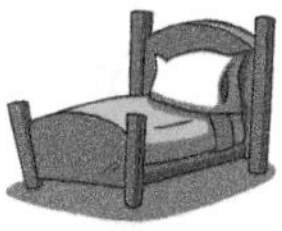 __ e __

4  wi __ __ ow

5  ha __ __

6  __ __ air

❺ Talk to a friend about the house in task 3.

This is the bedroom. There's a mirror too.

1 29 Listen, point and sing.

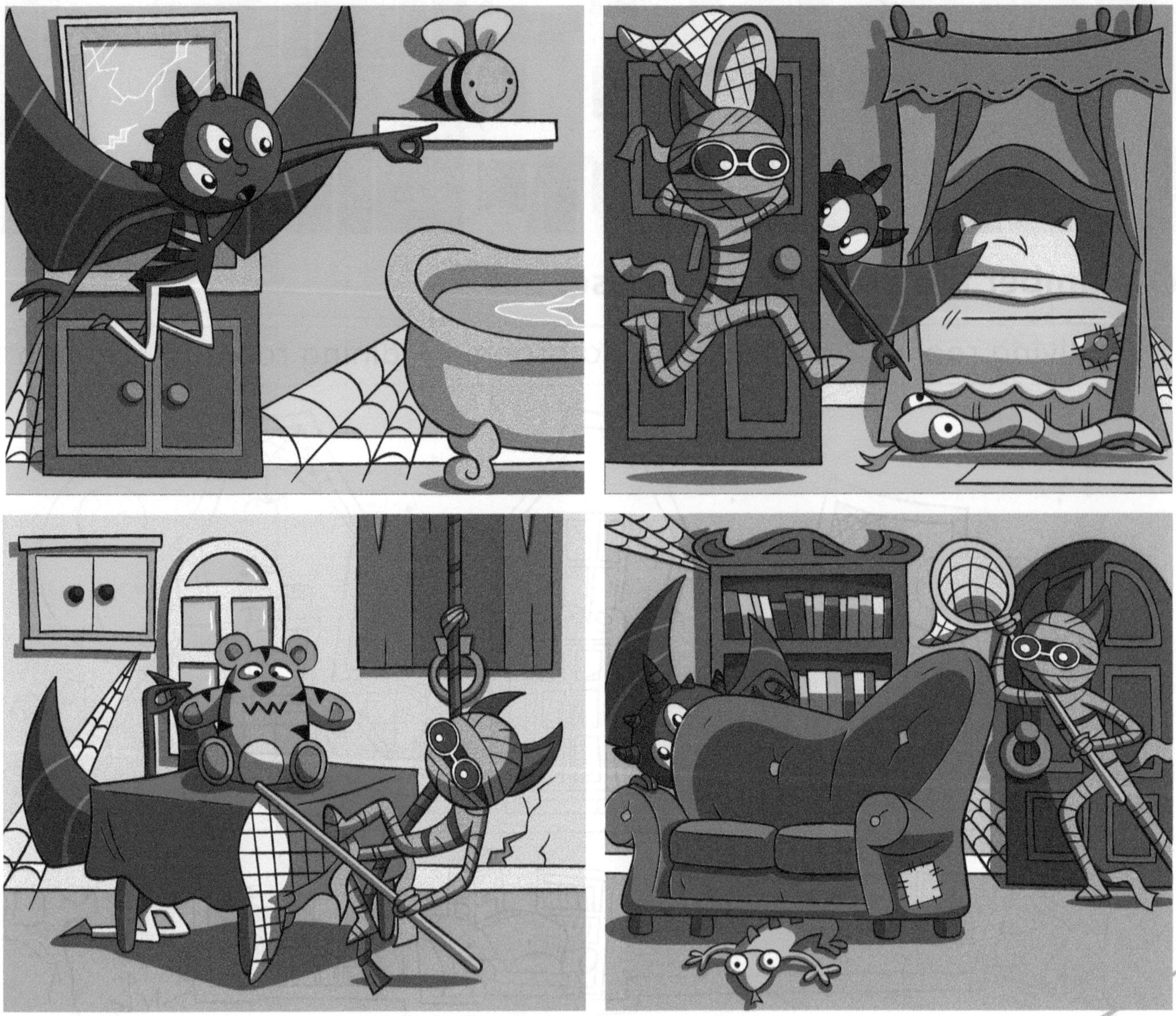

There's a bee in
the bathroom!
What can I do?
Don't worry.
I'm coming!
I can help you!

There's a snake in
the bedroom!
What can I do?
Don't worry!
I'm coming!
I can help you!

There's a tiger in
the kitchen!
What can I do?
Don't worry!
I'm coming!
I can help you!

There's a lizard in
the living room!
What can I do?
Don't worry!
I'm coming!
I can help you!

Let's see! What animals can
you find in your house?

2 30 Listen, point and colour.

3 Look at the picture in task 2. Read and tick (✓) the true sentences..

1 There's a bee on the clock. ____
2 There's a spider under the sofa. ____
3 There's a phone on the table. ____
4 There's a box under the sofa. ____
5 There's a lizard on the rug. ____
6 There's a camera on the bookcase. ____

4 Choose three objects in the picture in task 2. Tell your friend to find them.

Skills: Speaking, Writing

1 What can you see in the picture? Talk to a friend.

Mark: ___ / 7

2 Look at the picture in task 1 again. Write.

1 The plane is ________ .
2 The cars are yellow, ________ and ________ .
3 The ________ is white.
4 The school bus is________ .
5 The ________ is green.
6 The helicopter is ________ and ________ .

Mark: ___ / 8

3 Match and write.

1 Sue
2 Matt
3 Ann
4 Nick
5 Jill

1 Sue goes to school by ________ .
2 Matt goes to school ________________ .
3 Ann goes to ________________ .
4 Nick goes ________________ .
5 Jill ________________ .

Mark: ___ / 5

Total: ___ ___ / 20

Skills: Writing, Reading, Listening

1 Look and write.

kitchen living room dining room bedroom bathroom

Mark: ___ / 5

2 Look at the picture in task 1 again. Choose the correct words.

1 There is a **mat** / **clock** in the bathroom.

2 There are **two mirrors** / **two baths** in the house.

3 There is a **chair** / **window** in the hall.

4 There is a **phone** / **radio** in the dining room.

5 There are two **chairs** / **TVs** in the living room.

Mark: ___ / 5

3 31 Listen and draw.

Mark: ___ / 7

Total: ___ ___ / 17

11 A great day!

1 Moyo has breakfast in the ________ .

2 He goes to his grandma's house in the ________ .

3 He has a birthday party in the ________ .

4 He goes to sleep at ________ .

What a great day!

1 Look and write. What does Moyo do?

afternoon   evening   morning   night

2 Listen to Moyo and his cousin Grace. Write *yes* or *no*.

Example It's Grace's birthday. ____no____

1 Moyo opens a present. ________

2 The present is a book. ________

3 Moyo likes his present. ________

4 Moyo's favourite colour is green. ________

3 Read and match.

1 Every day, Moyo goes
2 He listens
3 He eats
4 He plays
5 He does
6 He reads

A a story at night.
B to his teacher in class.
C games in the afternoon.
D lunch at 1 o'clock.
E his homework in the evening.
F to school in the morning.

4 What does your friend do every day? Ask and answer. Then write.

in the morning	in the afternoon	in the evening	at night
have breakfast	______	______	______
______	______	______	______
______	______	______	______
______	______	______	______

1 Look and answer the questions.

1 Where is Moyo? in the ____________
2 What is he eating? ____________
3 What is he drinking? ____________

2 Look and match.

dinner

bed

TV

book

football

3 Read and write. Use words from task 2.

Hi Moyo,
This is what I do on Saturdays.
I play 1) ____________ in the afternoon.
Then I watch 2) ____________ .
I read a 3) ____________ with my dad.
I have 4) ____________ with my family in the evening.
Then I go to 5) ____________ at eight o'clock.
What do you do?

See you soon!
Grace

4 Look at the pictures. Where are they? Are they happy?

5 Look at the pictures in task 4 again. Answer each question with one word.

Picture 1

Example Where is the girl? in the *living room*

1 Who is she with? her ________

2 What are they doing? reading a ________

3 What is the boy doing? playing with a ________

4 Who is angry? the ________

Picture 2

5 Where is the boy sitting now? on the ________

6 What are the girl and the boy doing? listening to a ________

6 Talk to a friend.

12 Hobbies

❶ **Number photos 1–6. Use the words in the box.**

1 read **2** play **3** draw
4 listen to **5** fly **6** watch

❷ **Point to the photos. Talk to your friend.**

I like playing music.

I like drawing people.

❸ **What can you see? Complete the words.**

1 p __ nc __ l
2 m __ u __ e
3 c __ m __ r __
4 k __ t __
5 h __ l __ c __ pt __ r
6 r __ d __ __
7 c __ m __ c
8 s __ at __ b __ a __ d

4 Look at the picture. Answer the questions.

How many children are there? 8

1 Which children are playing instruments?

2 What colour is the kite?

3 What is Tom reading?

4 What is Nick painting?

5 Who is flying a helicopter?

5 33 Look at the picture in task 4 again. Listen and draw.

6 Listen and draw.

Say one word and tell your friend where to draw it in the picture above. Take turns.

ball bike book car doll guitar TV plane robot kite

Draw a car next to the trees.

Draw a guitar on the grass.

❶ **Read and write.**

board games | songs | radio | books | kites

The hobbies song

I like reading (1) ______

and singing (2) ______.

I like listening to the (3) ______ too!

I like flying (4) ______

Playing (5) ______

Do you like these things too?

❷ 34 **Listen and check your answers. Sing the song.**

❸ 35 **Listen to the children talking about their hobbies. Number the pictures.**

A

B

C

D

4 Complete the hobby survey. Ask and answer with a friend.

	DO YOU LIKE ...?		ME	MY CLASSMATE
1		painting	no	yes
2		playing ______ ______ .		
3		playing ______ ______		
4		playing the ______ .		
5		reading ______		

5 Make a graph of your class hobbies.

6 Look at the graph. Write about your friends' hobbies.

In my class ...

1 ______ children like painting.

2 ______ children like ______ .

3 ______ children ______ .

4 ______ children ______ .

5 ______ children ______ .

Review Unit 11

Skills: Reading, Listening, Speaking

1 Match.

1	have	A	homework
2	watch	B	a story
3	do	C	breakfast
4	play	D	to bed
5	read	E	my bike
6	go	F	TV
7	ride	G	games

Mark: ___ / 7

2 (36) Listen and draw the time.

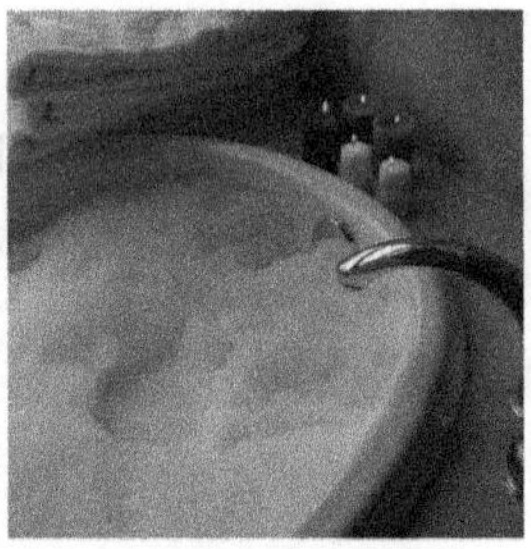

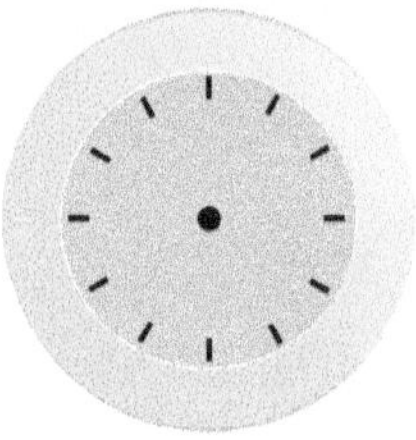
play basketball

go to my grandpa's house

go to the beach

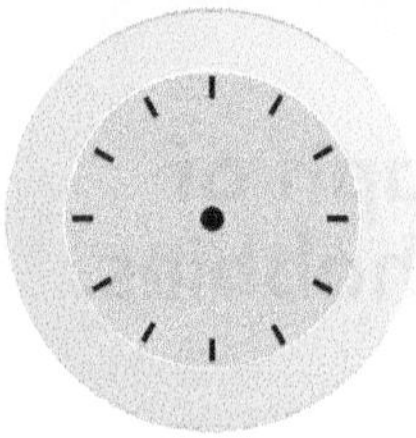
have a bath

have lunch

Mark: ___ / 5

3 Look at the clocks. What time is it? What do you do at that time?

It's 10 o'clock in the morning. I listen to my teacher.

Mark: ___ / 8

Total: ___ / 20

Skills: Writing, Reading

1 Complete the phrases.

draw fly listen to ~~play~~ read watch

Example play the guitar 1 ______ a book 2 ______ the radio

3 ______ a helicopter 4 ______ TV 5 ______ a picture

Mark: ___ / 5

2 Look and read. Put a tick (✓) or a cross (✗).

	Lucy likes drawing.	✓
1	She likes listening to the radio.	
2	She likes playing computer games.	
3	Dan likes taking photos.	
4	He likes reading comic books.	
5	He likes riding a bike.	

Mark: ___ / 5

3 What do you like doing in your free time? Write.

1 I like ______.
2 I like ______.
3 I ______.
4 I ______.

Mark: ___ / 8
Total: ___ / 18

Songs and chants

Unit 1 page 7

5 3 **Listen to the song and do the actions.**

We go to school in the morning.
Let's start the day!
It's English class.
Hip, hip hooray!

Hello, teacher!
Hello, friends!
How are you today?
I'm fine, thank you.

We go to school in the morning.
Let's learn English!
Let's have fun!
We love to learn and play!
Hip, hip hooray!

Unit 3 page 19

4 13 **Listen and chant.**

Look at my robot!
It's got three arms and four legs.
Has it got small feet? Yes, it has!

This is my robot.
I like it a lot!

Look at my robot!
It likes cleaning. It likes painting.
It likes walking and talking.

This is my robot.
I like it a lot!

Unit 5, page 27

5 16 **Listen and chant.**

Sh, sh, sh!
Say with me
Sh, sh, sh
1, 2, 3
shirt ...shoes... T-shirt

Unit 6, page 30

2 18 **Listen, point and sing.**

It's time for breakfast.
What can you see?
Milk, bread and fruit too!
I love milk! Me too!

It's time for lunch.
What can you see?
Fish, chips and beans too!
I love chips! Me too!

It's time for dinner.
What can you see?
Rice, chicken and carrots too!
I love rice! Me too!

Songs and chants

Unit 8, page 41

7 25 **Sing and act out.**

We're having fun at school today.
Let's have a good time!
We're skateboarding,
We're jumping up high
We're swimming!
Sports for everyone!

We're having fun at school today.
Let's have a good time!
We're kicking a ball,
We're bouncing a ball,
We're throwing a ball!
Sports for everyone!

Unit 9, page 48

1 27 **Listen and sing. Write the words.**

Hurry, hurry
Don't be late!
It's time to go
to school!

drive in a car

ride a bike

walk with friends

ride a horse

ride a bus

fly in a blue plane

Hurry, hurry
Don't be late!
It's time to go
to school!

Unit 10, page 52

7 29 **Sing and act out.**

There's a bee
in the bathroom!
What can I do?
Don't worry.
I'm coming!
I can help you!

There's a snake
in the bedroom!
What can I do?
Don't worry!
I'm coming!
I can help you!

There's a tiger
in the kitchen!
What can I do?
Don't worry!
I'm coming!
I can help you!

There's a lizard
in the living room!
What can I do?
Don't worry!
I'm coming!
I can help you!

Unit 12, page 62

2 34 **Listen and sing.**

I like reading books
and singing songs.
I like listening to the radio too!

I like flying kites
and playing board games
I like listening to the radio too!
Do you, do you, do you like these things too?

Unit 1

This is / These are with singular and regular plural nouns

This is a crayon. **This isn't** a tablet.	
These are crayons. **These aren't** tablets.	
Is this a tablet? **Are these** tablets?	

isn't = is not
aren't = are not

1 Complete the table.

One …	Two …
poster	posters
________	windows
desk	________
________	classrooms
bookcase	________
________	boards

2 Complete the sentences.

Are Is These ~~This~~ This

Example __This__ is a teacher.

1 ________ are pupils.
2 ________ this a new game?
3 ________ is a wall.
4 ________ these new computers?

Unit 2

There is / There are with regular and irregular plural nouns

There is a **child** in my family.
There isn't a **child** in my family.
Is there a **child** in your family?

There are two **children** in my family.
There aren't two **children** in my family.
Are there two **children** in your family?

1 Complete the table.

One …	Two …
________	children
person	________
________	women
man	________

2 Choose the correct words.

Example **There is / There are** three **child / children** in my family – me, my sister and my brother.

1 **There is / There are** two **woman / women** in the photo – my mother and my grandmother.
2 **There is / There are** four **window / windows** in my classroom.
3 **There is / There are** one **pet / pets** in my house – my dog, Barney.
4 **Is there / Are there** two **child / children** in your family?
5 **Is there / Are there** a **desk / desks** in your house?

Unit 3

Have (got)

I / You / We / They**'ve got** yellow feet. He / She / It**'s got** green legs. I / You / We / They **haven't got** pink feet. He / She / It **hasn't got** blue legs.	

've got = have got
haven't got = have not got
hasn't got = has not got

1 Complete the sentences.

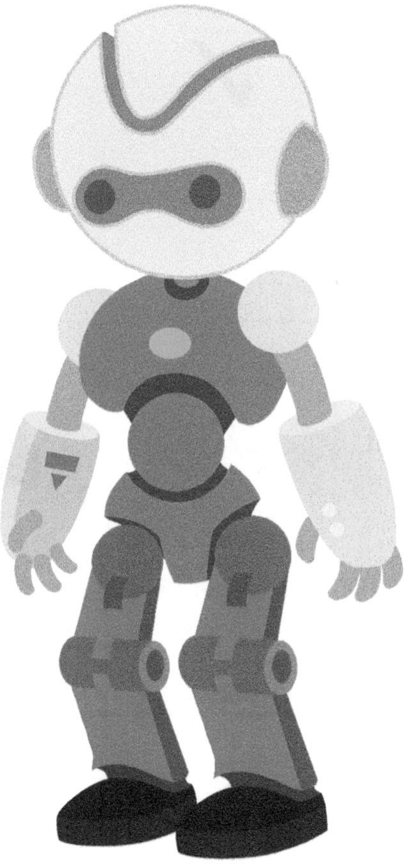

Example The robot _'s got_ two green arms.

1 It ______ a blue body.
2 It ______ yellow legs.
3 It ______ a purple head.
4 It ______ black feet.

Unit 4

There is / There are (questions and short answers)

Is there a cat in the picture?	Yes, **there is.** No, **there isn't.**
Are there some cats in the picture?	**Yes, there are.** No, **there aren't.**
How many cats **are there?**	**There's** one **cat.** **There are** two **cats.**

there's = there is   aren't = are not

1 Look. Count and write.

Example _There's one_ desk.

1 ______ bookshelves.
2 ______ poster.
3 ______ bed.
4 ______ dolls.
5 ______ robots.

2 Look at the picture again. Match the questions to the answers.

Example Are there any bookshelves?	A Yes, there is.
1 Is there a desk?	B No, there isn't.
2 Is there a window?	C Yes, there are.
3 Are there any fish?	D No, there aren't.

Unit 5

Present continuous

I'm (not) wear**ing** a red T-shirt. He / She / It **is** (not) wear**ing** a T-shirt. You / We / They **are** (not) wear**ing** a T-shirt.	
What am I wear**ing**? **What are** you / we / they wear**ing**? **What's** he / she / it wear**ing**?	
Am I wear**ing** a red T-shirt? ***Is*** he / she / it wear***ing*** a red T-shirt? **Are** you / we / they wear**ing** a red T-shirt?	Yes, I **am**. Yes, he / she / it **is**. Yes, you / we / they **are**. No, **I'm not**. No, he / she / it's **not**. No, you / we / they**'re not**.

I'm = I am   What's = What is

1 Write sentences.

Example (Alex / wear / green trousers)
Alex is wearing green trousers.

1 (Eva / not play / in the garden)
____

2 (Abdullah / eat / an egg)
____

3 (I / not sing / a song)
____

4 (Hugo and Jill / watch TV)
____

2 Write the answers.

Example **A:** Is she wearing purple trousers?
B: Yes, she is.

1 **A:** Is he wearing a blue T-shirt?
B: No, ______________________.

2 **A:** Are they listening to music?
B: Yes, ______________________.

3 **A:** Are you playing with the cat?
B: No, ______________________.

4 **A:** Are you running in the playground?
B: Yes, ______________________.

Unit 6

like / love with *Me too! / So do I!*

✓	
I / We / You / They **like** eggs.	I / We / You / They **love** apples.
He / She / It **likes** eggs.	He / She / It **loves** apples.

I love cake.	Me too! So do I!

1 Look and write.

	✓	
Grandma		
Mum and Dad		
You and Sarah	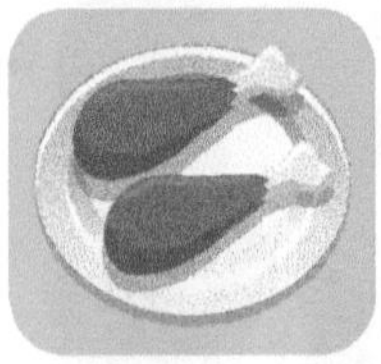	

Example Grandma likes milk, but she loves orange juice.

1 Mum and Dad __________ bananas, but they __________ grapes.

2 Sarah __________ chicken, but she __________ fish – and so __________ I!

3 **A:** I like chicken.
B: Me __________ !

Unit 7

Adjectives

Adjective + noun
It's a **fantastic day.** He's a **funny boy.** They're **beautiful photos.** I've got a **new hat.**
***be* + adjective**
I'm hungry. The man **is angry.** The table **isn't clean.** **Are** the gates **open?**

It's = It is
He's = He is
They're = They are

1 Match the opposites.

Example big → C	A happy
1 new	B open
2 clean	C small
3 closed	D old
4 sad	E dirty

2 Order the words.

Example ride. / a / scary / It's
It's a scary ride.

1 old / man. / an / He's

____

2 favourite / is / my / This / T-shirt.

____

3 beautiful. / photos / The / are

____

4 The / dirty. / is / table

____

5 dog / or small? / Is / big / the

____

Unit 8

Question word *whose* with possessive 's

Whose ball is it? **Whose** is it?	It's Anna's (ball).
Whose toys are they? **Whose** are they?	They're Ben's (toys).

1 Look and write.

1 It's ________ skateboard.

2 It's ________ football.

3 They're ________ flowers.

2 Write questions with *whose*.

Example A: *Whose teddy is it?*
B: It's May's teddy.

1 A: ______________________________ ?
B: It's Grandpa's hat.

2 A: ______________________________ ?
B: They're Antonio's chips.

3 A: ______________________________ ?
B: It's Grace's skirt.

4 A: ______________________________ ?
B: They're Bill's glasses.

Unit 9

Possessive adjectives

Possessive adjective + noun
I go to school with **my mum**.
Is this **your house**?
The boy rides **his bike**.
The woman drives **her lorry**.
The robot lives in **its cupboard**.
We fly in **our helicopter**.
Sue and Alex ride **their bikes**.

1 Choose the correct words.

Example The girl lives with **its / her** brother. (her circled)

1 My brother likes **his / her** scooter.

2 We like playing with **our / their** dog in the garden.

3 They fly in **their / your** helicopter to the beach.

4 The alien is looking for **their / its** friends.

2 Write.

Example This is my grandma. Her name's Christina.

1 I'm wearing ________ hat because I'm at the beach.

2 My friends and I ride ________ bikes to school.

3 The monster is bouncing ________ ball.

4 Hello, what's ________ name?

Unit 10

Let's

***Let's* + verb**
Let's see.
Let's colour the picture.
Let's play a game.

1 Read and look. Match.

Example Let's find a tiger.

1 Let's go to my apartment.

2 Let's take some photos.

3 Let's go to the beach.

4 Let's play baseball.

A 

B 

C 

D 

E 

2 Order the words.

Example ride / let's / our / bikes
Let's ride our bikes.

1 house / let's / the / clean

____

2 eat / let's / dining room / in / the

____

3 the / play / let's / in / living room

____

4 sit / the / on / sofa / let's

____

Grammar fun!

Unit 11

Prepositions of time

at night **at** five o'clock
in the morning / the afternoon / the evening

1 Complete the sentences.

Example Let's have dinner __*at*__ seven o'clock.

1 May goes home ________ the afternoon.

2 Matt and Mehdi like reading books ________ night.

3 I start school ________ eight o'clock ________ the morning.

4 We play board games ________ the evening.

5 He wakes up early ________ the morning.

2 Look and write.

Example

I go to sleep __*at ten o'clock*__.

1  I go to school ________.

2  We eat dinner________.

3 

They go to the beach ________.

4 

Let's play baseball ________.

Unit 12

Like + verb + *-ing*

I / You / We / They **like** draw**ing**. He / She / It **likes** draw**ing**.
I / You / We / They **don't like** draw**ing**. He / She / It **doesn't like** draw**ing**.
Do I / you / we / they **like** draw**ing**? Does he / she / it **like** draw**ing**?

don't = do not doesn't = does not

1 Complete the sentences.

Example My brother __*likes running*__ with his friends. (like, run)

1 I ________ the kitchen. (not like, clean)

2 She ________ her kite in the park. (like, fly)

3 We ________ to music in my room. (like, listen)

4 He ________ in the evening. (not like, drive)

2 Look and complete the sentences.

Lucy and Matt	 play the guitar	 draw

1 Lucy and Matt ________, but they ________.

Have (got) for characteristics (Unit 3)

1 Tell your partner about one of the people. *Use have (got)*. Who is it?

Leon
Bobbie
Frankie
Max
a classmate
a teacher

Example: He's got green arms and legs. He's got black hands and feet. He's got a black tail and blue ears. It's Captain Zoom!

There is / There are, nouns (Units 2 & 4)

2 Talk with your partner about your picture.

Listen and draw your partner's picture.
Student B: look at page 77.

Example:
- There are some cats.
- How many cats are there?
- There are two cats.

So do I / Me too! (Unit 6)

3 Tell your partner what you like. Listen to your partner and say *So do I / Me too*! if you agree.

Student B: look at page 77.

football robots
giraffes carrots
school

Example:
- I like football ... I like robots.
- Me too!

Prepositions of time (Unit 11)

4 Ask your partner the questions. Fill in Nedda's calendar.

Listen to your partner and answer.
Student B: look at page 77.

When does she sing songs?
When does she clean the house?
When does she study at school?
When does she read books?
When does she draw pictures?

Example:
- When does she sing songs?
- She sings songs on Friday, at 3 o'clock in the afternoon.

	Monday	Tuesday	Wednesday	Thursday	Friday
Morning		- Listen to music – 11 o'clock			- Ride a bike – 8 o'clock
Afternoon				- Go to sleep – 2 o'clock	
Evening		- Play tennis – 6 o'clock		- Play tennis – 7 o'clock	- Look at the moon – 10 o'clock

Grammar fun pairwork!

Let's (Unit 10)

1 Look and make sentences. Use *Let's* and the words in the box.

go to bed	take a picture
play tennis	run fast
drink some water	

Student B

There is / There are, nouns (Units 2 & 4)

2 Talk with your partner about your picture.

Listen and draw your partner's picture. Student A: look at page 76.

Example: - *There are some people.*
- *How many people are there?*
- *There are seven people.*

So do I / Me too! (Unit 6)

3 Tell your partner what you like. Listen to your partner and say *So do I / Me too!* if you agree.

Student A: look at page 76.

skateboarding	teddy bears
monkeys	fruit
the playground	

Example: - *I like skateboarding ...*
I like teddy bears.
- *Me too!*

Prepositions of time (Unit 11)

4 Ask your partner the questions. Fill in Captain Zoom's calendar. Listen to your partner and answer.

Student A: look at page 76.

When does he listen to music?
When does he look at the moon?
When does he play tennis?
When does he ride a bike?
When does he go to sleep?

Example: - *When does he listen to music?*
- *He listens to music on Tuesday, at 11 o'clock in the morning.*

	Monday	Tuesday	Wednesday	Thursday	Friday
Morning	- Study at school – 9 o'clock		- Study at school – 10 o'clock		
Afternoon	- Draw pictures – 3 o'clock	- Clean the house – 1 o'clock	- Read books – 2 o'clock	- Go to sleep – 2 o'clock	- Sing songs – 3 o'clock
Evening					

Listening Checklist

Circle (magic squirrel), if your answer is Yes!

- I can recognise English names when I hear them.
- I listened to a song and did the right actions in task 5 on page 7.
- I can draw lines to match names to people in a picture.
- I listened to Jacob talking about his pet and circled the right answers in task 3 on page 23.
- I can write down the numbers I hear.
- I matched the descriptions I heard of how people were dressed to the right pictures in task 2 on page 28.
- I can listen to a spelling and write it down with no mistakes.
- I coloured the things in the room correctly in task 2 on page 53.
- I can follow my teacher's instructions when she speaks in English.
- I played the game in task 6 on page 61 and put the pictures in the right place.

How many magic squirrels did you get?

Reading & Writing Checklist

Check your progress, colour the stars!

	OK	Great
I can write clearly in English.		
I can unjumble letters to spell the picture words correctly.		
I can copy words without making mistakes.		
I can read and write more than five animals.		
I can read and understand short sentences about a picture.		
I can fill gaps in a text from a choice of words.		
I can read and write more than five things in the house.		
I can write 'yes' or 'no' to say if a sentence about a picture is true.		
I can read and write more than five sports.		
I like reading stories with pictures in English.		

Reading & Writing Checklist

Circle , if your answer is Yes!

I chose the correct words for things in a classroom to match the pictures in task 3 on page 7.

I knew the correct plurals of the words in task 5 on page 11.

I liked writing about my robot in task 2 on page 18.

I chose the correct answers about how many animals are on the farm in task 4 on page 21.

I can spell the clothes words in task 3 on page 28.

I unjumbled the food words correctly in task 3 on page 30.

I chose the correct question words in task 2 on page 39.

I matched the correct sentences to the pictures of sports in task 4 on page 41.

I wrote about my home in task 2 on page 50.

I put the correct words in the gaps in the sentences about Grace's day in task 3 on page 58.

How many magic squirrels did you get?

Speaking Checklist

Check your progress, colour the stars!

	OK	Great
I can say hello and tell someone my name clearly in English.		
I said how to spell my name and wrote my friend's name when I heard it in task 3 on page 8.		
I can point to things in a picture when someone asks me to.		
I talked about the picture of the classroom in task 5 on page 19.		
I can understand simple spoken questions.		
I said all the sports words clearly in task 3 on page 40.		
I can talk about myself in English.		
I asked and answered questions about travelling in task 5 on page 47.		
I am not scared if someone speaks English to me.		
I asked my friend about favourite hobbies in task 4 on page 63.		

Word list

Unit 1

basketball *n* ________

black *adj* ________

blue *adj* ________

board *n* ________

classroom *n* ________

computer *n* ________

cupboard *n* ________

desk *n* ________

football *n* ________

green *adj* ________

hello ________

line *n* ________

listen *v* ________

look *v* ________

love *v* ________

morning *n* ________

no ________

number *n* ________

photo *n* ________

picture *n* ________

pink *adj* ________

play *v* ________

playground *n* ________

poster *n* ________

read *v* ________

red *adj* ________

school *n* ________

song *n* ________

tablet *n* ________

talk *v* ________

teacher *n* ________

window *n* ________

write *v* ________

Unit 2

baby *n* ________

boy *n* ________

child (children) *n* ________

dog *n* ________

family *n* ________

girl *n* ________

grandfather *n* ________

grandmother *n* ________

house *n* ________

man *n* ________

pet *n* ________

woman (women) *n* ________

Unit 3

arm *n* ________

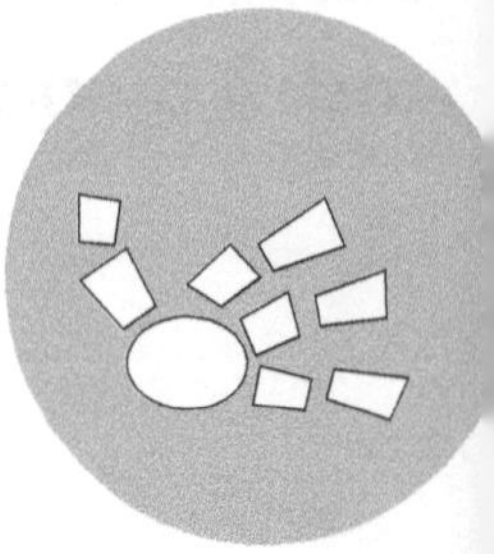

body *n* ________

colour *n+v* ________

foot (feet) *n* ________

hand *n* ________

head *n* ____________

leg *n* ____________

painting *n* ____________

robot *n* ____________

Unit 4

box *n* ____________

chicken *n* ____________

cow *n* ____________

cross *n+v* ____________

duck *n* ____________

frog *n* ____________

goat *n* ____________

lizard *n* ____________

mouse *n* ____________

sheep *n* ____________

tick *n+v* ____________

Unit 5

baseball cap *n* ____________

bedroom *n* ____________

boots *n* ____________

chair *n* ____________

clothes *n* ____________

dress *n* ____________

glasses *n* ____________

hat *n* ____________

jacket *n* ____________

jeans *n* ____________

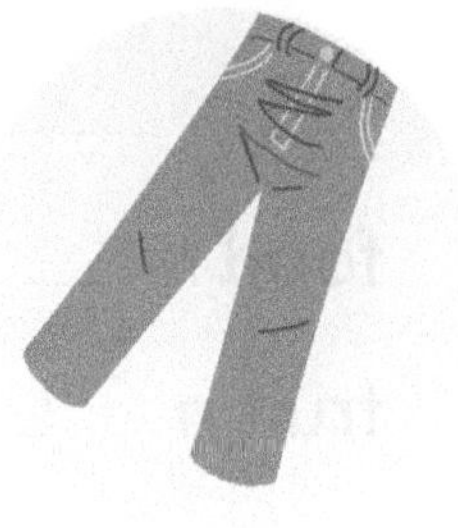

orange *adj* ____________

point *v* ____________

shirt *n* ____________

shoe *n* ____________

shorts *n* ____________

skirt *n* ____________

socks *n* ____________

trousers *n* ____________

T-shirt *n* ____________

white *adj* ____________

Unit 6

apple *n* ____________

banana *n* ____________

beans *n* ____________

bread n ____________

breakfast *n* ____________

cake *n* ____________

carrot *n* ____________

chicken *n* ____________

chips *n* ____________

dinner *n* ____________

drink *n+v* ____________

ear *n* ____________

egg *n* ____________

eye *n* ____________

fish *n* ________

food *n* ________
fruit *n* ________
grapes *n* ________

hair *n* ________
heart *n* ________
juice *n* ________
kiwi *n* ________
lunch *n* ________
milk *n* ________
mouth *n* ________

nose *n* ________
rice *n* ________
yellow *adj* ________

Unit 7

angry *adj* ________
ball *n* ________

balloon *n* ________
boat *n* ________
book *n* ________
brown *adj* ________
happy *adj* ________
ice cream *n* ________
lamp *n* ________
sad *adj* ________

scary *adj* ________

train *n* ________
tree *n* ________

Unit 8

alien *n* ________

baseball *n* ________
bat *n* ________
bounce *v* ________
doll *n* ________
door *n* ________

flower *n* ________
football *n* ________
hockey *n* ________

jump *v* ________
kick *v* ________
monster *n* ________
sand *n* ________
skateboard *n* ________
sport *n* ________

swim *v* ________
table *n* ________
table tennis *n* ________

teddy bear *n* ________
tennis (racket) *n* ________
throw *v* ________
water *n* ________

Unit 9

beach *n* ____________

bike *n* ____________

bus *n* ____________

car *n* ____________

helicopter *n* ____________

lorry *n* ____________

motorbike *n* ____________

plane *n* ____________

train *n* ____________

Unit 10

bathroom *n* ____________

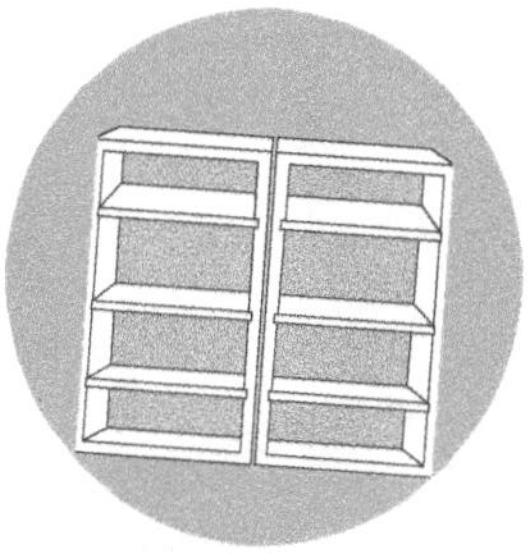

bed *n* ____________

bee *n* ____________

bookcase *n* ____________

camera *n* ____________

clock *n* ____________

dining room *n* ____________

flat *n* ____________

hall *n* ____________

kitchen *n* ____________

living room *n* ____________

rug *n* ____________

mirror *n* ____________

phone *n+v* ____________

sing *v* ____________

snake *n* ____________

sofa *n* ____________

spider *n* ____________

tiger *n* ____________

Unit 11

afternoon *n* ____________

birthday *n* ____________

eat *v* ____________

evening *n* ____________

morning *n* ____________

night *n* ____________

sit *v* ____________

sleep *v* ____________

story *n* ____________

teacher *n* ____________

TV *n* ____________

Unit 12

board game *n* ____________

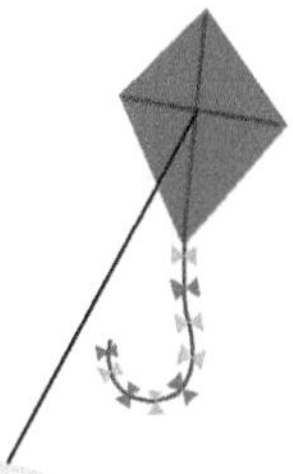

(computer) mouse *n* ____________

guitar *n* ____________

kite *n* ____________

music *n* ____________

park *n* ____________

pencil *n* ____________

radio *n* ____________

In your book ...

Nedda

Likes: puppies, videos, drawing, spaghetti, the moon, unicorns

Dislikes: sharks, lions, aliens, broccoli

Captain Zoom

Likes: sports, snow, skating, caves

Dislikes:: girls, water, dancing, umbrellas

Bobbie

Likes: carrot, music, eggs, apples, running, dancing, pears, grapes

Dislikes:: candy, riding bikes, lettuce, oranges

Leon

Likes: friends, gum

Dislikes: blood, scary things

Piper

Likes: flying, reading stories

Dislikes: walking, hats, boots

Frankie

Likes: fashion, pink, bed, hugs

Dislikes: soup

... from kids around the world

Alejandra, 8

Hugo, 8

Julia, 8

Luiźa, 7

Alan, 6

Anna, 7

Jesse

Likes: flying, burritos, spiders, dancing, red, eating

Dislikes: mushrooms, yellow, cats, black

Checklist buddy

Likes: pizza, apple juice, playing ball

Dislikes: ice cream, burgers, mice, cats

Exam Professor

Likes: science, music, interesting animals, playing basketball

Dislikes: disorder, meat, destruction, black

Max

Likes: balloons, bananas, apples

Dislikes: cleaning my room

Think Big Giraffe

Likes: plants

Dislikes: meat

Sage

Likes: reading, eating, joking, art

Dislikes: pickles, flies, the dark, cockroaches

Aurora, 9

Luisa, 7

Mariya, 8

Mario, 11

Adriana, 7

Edith, 11

Author acknowledgements

Claire Medwell would like to give thanks to the editorial team for all their help and support throughout the writing process and to her children who provide an endless source of inspiration.

Adam Scott would like to thank Ann-Marie and Lynn for their faultless support, his co-author for her help and guidance, and Ed for being there through it all.

Publisher acknowledgements

The authors and publishers are grateful to the following for reviewing the material during the writing process:

Georgia Forte, Polly Gittens: Italy; Nadezda Volkova: Spain; Muruvvet Celik: Turkey; Maritza Suarez Gonzalez: Mexico.

Acknowledgements

The authors and publishers acknowledge the following sources of copyright material and are grateful for the permissions granted. While every effort has been made, it has not always been possible to identify the sources of all the material used, or to trace all copyright holders. If any omissions are brought to our notice, we will be happy to include the appropriate acknowledgements on reprinting & in the next update to the digital edition, as applicable.

Key: U = Unit.

Photography

The following photographs are sourced from Getty Images.

U1: Inti St Clair; Steve Prezant/Corbis; kali9/E+; Blend Images - Kris Timken; goldenKB/iStock/Getty Images Plus; FatCamera/E+; Steve Debenport/E+; **U2:** Terry Vine/DigitalVision; Ariel Skelley/DigitalVision; Wayne R Bilenduke/The Image Bank; MStudioImages/E+; Juanmonino/iStock/Getty Images Plus; Ashley Cooper/Corbis NX; Eternity in an Instant/DigitalVision; Amanda Hall/robertharding; IgorSPb/iStock/Getty Images Plus; Emmanuelle Bonzami/EyeEm; Kevin Kozicki/Image Source; Lisa Peardon/The Image Bank; Alex Wilson/Photodisc; Samig Mung-Aroon/EyeEm; **U3:** Maciej Frolow/Photographer's Choice RF; Donald Iain Smith/Photodisc; bulentgultek/E+; KOHb/iStock/Getty Images Plus; pleshko74/iStock/Getty Images Plus; **U4:** Ridofranz/iStock/Getty Images Plus; Blend Images - JGI/Jamie Grill; BJI/Blue Jean Images; Cyndi Monaghan/Moment; Libardo Lambrano/500px; Barry Miller/EyeEm; Christian Peters/iStock/Getty Images Plus; simonlong/Moment; Steve Prezant/Corbis; **U5:** Andy Crawford/Dorling Kindersley; sturti/E+; PeopleImages/E+; RichVintage/E+; Esther Moreno Martinez/EyeEm; jabejon/iStock/Getty Images Plus; **U6:** View Stock; John Carey/Photolibrary/Getty Images Plus; manyakotic/iStock/Getty Images Plus; asiseeit/E+; BJI/Blue Jean Images; imagestock/E+; lushmedia/E+; Claudia Totir/Moment; Lionel Ng/Moment Open; George Coppock/Photolibrary; Maximilian Stock Ltd/Photolibrary; a_namenko/iStock/Getty Images Plus; Dash_med/iStock/Getty Images Plus; PeopleImages/iStock/Getty Images Plus; Dorling Kindersley: Dave King; Jose Luis Pelaez Inc/DigitalVision; Caiaimage/Chris Ryan; Bill Sykes/Cultura; Wavebreakmedia/iStock/Getty Images Plus; **U7:** Flashpop/DigitalVision; jsteck/E+; Rivers Dale/Image Source; Elva Etienne/Moment; Lisa Taggart/EyeEm; RyanJLane/E+; Radius Images; **U8:** Shoji Fujita/DigitalVision; FatCamera/E+; PeopleImages/E+; Paul Blackley/Moment; Sollina Images; Pollyana FMS; Jose Luis Pelaez/Corbis/VCG; Santiago Urquijo/Moment; Tetra Images; Indeed; Cultura RM Exclusive/Christine Schneider; Jose Luis Pelaez Inc/DigitalVision; Lauren Burke/Photographer's Choice; joecicak/iStock/Getty Images Plus; Dorling Kindersley; Susanna Price/Dorling Kindersley; John Kroetch; sitox/E+; Nicolò Campo/LightRocket; Jose Luis Pelaez Inc/Digital Vision; Hoxton/Tom Merton; Ariel Skelley/DigitalVision; **U9:** Vladimiroquai/iStock/Getty Images Plus; Dave King/Dorling Kindersley; Bernard Roussel/Photographer's Choice; Light Thru My Lens Photography/Moment; Studio 504/Stone; Felix Behnke/Cultura; Ridofranz/iStock/Getty Images Plus; Siyi Huang/EyeEm; Imgorthand/E+; Colorblind Images LLC/DigitalVision; Bauer-Griffin/GC Images; Westend61; Siyi Huang/EyeEm; **U10:** Alina Nasibulina/EyeEm; Ryan McVay/Photodisc; Jupiterimages/Stockbyte; Klaus Vedfelt/DigitalVision; tatyana_tomsickova/iStock/Getty Images Plus; Tobias Lindner/EyeEm; hadynyah/E+; Shoji Fujita/DigitalVision; Sappington Todd; nycshooter/E+; Vstock; PeterAustin/E+; **U11:** asiseeit/E+; AL Hedderly/Moment; AlexRaths/iStock/Getty Images Plus; gbh007/iStock/Getty Images Plus; Image Source; ksalt/iStock/Getty Images Plus; Vyacheslav Argenberg (www.vascoplanet.com)/Moment; Alistair Berg/DigitalVision; **U12:** Milan_Jovic/E+; Hendrata Yoga Surya/EyeEm; Manabu Ogasawara/Stockbyte; Steve Gorton/Dorling Kindersley; rocketegg/iStock/Getty Images Plus; Jobalou/DigitalVision Vectors; Carol Yepes/Moment; Peter Dazeley/Photographer's Choice; Westend61; ArtMarie/E+; Colorblind Images LLC/DigitalVision; PeopleImages/E+; Michael H/DigitalVision; SetsukoN/iStock/Getty Images Plus; Olivier Cochet/EyeEm.

The following photograph is sourced from other library.

Tetra Images, LLC/Alamy Stock Photo.

Illustrations

Fran and David Brylewski (Beehive Illustration); Amanda Enright (Advocate Art); Pablo Gallego (Beehive Illustration); Leo Trinidad (The Bright Agency); Dave Williams (The Bright Agency); Collaborate Agency; Wild Apple Design Ltd.

Front cover illustrations by Collaborate Agency; Amanda Enright; Leo Trinidad; Jhonny Nunez; Pol Cunyat; Benedetta Capriotti; Dan Widdowson; Pand P Studio/Shuterstock; Piotr Urakau/Shuterstock.

Audio

Audio production by Ian Harker.

Chants by AmyJo Doherty and Martin Spangle.

Song composition and production (including some vocals) by Robert Lee at Dib Dib Dub Studios, UK.

Design

Design and typeset by Wild Apple Design Ltd

Cover design by Collaborate agency

Additional design layout EMC design Ltd